Straight Talk About...
SEXUAL ORIENTATION AND GENDER IDENTITY

Rachel Stuckey

Crabtree Publishing Company
www.crabtreebooks.com

Straight
Talk About...

Produced for Crabtree Publishing by:
Infinch Solutions

Publishing Director: Ravi Lakhina

Author: Rachel Stuckey

Project Controller: Vishal Obroi

Editors: John Perritano, Rebecca Sjonger

Proofreader: Shannon Welbourn

Art director: Dibakar Acharjee

Designer: Rajbir

Project coordinator: Kelly Spence

Production coordinator: Margaret Amy Salter

Prepress technician: Margaret Amy Salter

Consultant: Jessica Alcock, Residential Counselor BA Psychology, MA Child and Youth Studies

Photographs:
Cover: oneinchpunch/Thinkstock
Title page: mangostock/Shutterstock Inc.; p.4: Steve Pepple/Shutterstock Inc.; p.6: racorn/Shutterstock Inc.; p.8: ARZTSAMUI/Shutterstock Inc.; p.9: Stefano Tinti/Shutterstock Inc.; p.10: RyFlip/Shutterstock Inc.; p.12: Chepko Danil Vitalevich/Shutterstock Inc.; p.13: SOMMAI/Shutterstock Inc.; p.15: Cromagnon/Shutterstock Inc.; p.16: Eugenio Marongiu/Shutterstock Inc.; p.17: AJP/Shutterstock Inc.; p.18: littleny/Shutterstock Inc.; p.20: Grigoriev Ruslan/Shutterstock Inc.; p.21: bogdan ionescu/Shutterstock Inc.; p.22: Guas/Shutterstock Inc.; p.23: Monkey Business Images/Shutterstock Inc.; p.24: De Jongh Photography/Shutterstock Inc.; p.26: bikeriderlondon/Shutterstock Inc.; p.28: Kamira/Shutterstock Inc.; p.29: Atomazul/Shutterstock Inc.; p.30: Lisa F. Young/Shutterstock Inc.; p.32: Karin Hildebrand Lau/Shutterstock Inc.; p.34: maxriesgo/Shutterstock Inc.; p.35: lev radin/Shutterstock Inc.; p.36: Alon Brik/Shutterstock inc.; p.38: maximino/Shutterstock Inc.; p.39: Foto011/Shutterstock Inc.; p.40: Sabphoto/Shutterstock Inc.; p.42: aldegonde/Shutterstock Inc.; p.43: Jason Stitt/Shutterstock Inc.

Library and Archives Canada Cataloguing in Publication

Stuckey, Rachel, author
    Sexual orientation and gender identity / Rachel Stuckey.

(Straight talk about...)
Includes index.
Issued in print and electronic formats.
ISBN 978-0-7787-2203-8 (bound).--ISBN 978-0-7787-2207-6 (pbk.).--
ISBN 978-1-4271-9978-2 (pdf).--ISBN 978-1-4271-9974-4 (html)

    1. Sexual minorities--Juvenile literature. 2. Gender identity--
Juvenile literature. 3. Sexual orientation--Juvenile literature.
I. Title. II. Series: Straight talk about...

HQ76.26.S78 2015   j306.76'6   C2014-908101-4
                               C2014-908102-2

Library of Congress Cataloging-in-Publication Data

Stuckey, Rachel.
    Sexual orientation and gender identity / Rachel Stuckey.
      pages cm. -- (Straight talk about...)
    Includes index.
    ISBN 978-0-7787-2203-8 (reinforced library binding) --
ISBN 978-0-7787-2207-6 (pbk.) --
ISBN 978-1-4271-9978-2 (electronic pdf) --
ISBN 978-1-4271-9974-4 (electronic html)
    1. Sexual orientation--Juvenile literature. 2. Gender identity--
Juvenile literature. I. Title.

    HQ18.5.S78 2015
    306.76--dc23
                            2014045087

Crabtree Publishing Company

www.crabtreebooks.com   1-800-387-7650

Printed in Canada/022015/MA20150101

Published in Canada
Crabtree Publishing
616 Welland Ave.
St. Catharines, ON
L2M 5V6

Published in the United States
Crabtree Publishing
PMB 59051
350 Fifth Avenue, 59th Floor
New York, NY 10118

Published in the United Kingdom
Crabtree Publishing
Maritime House
Basin Road North, Hove
BN41 1WR

Published in Australia
Crabtree Publishing
3 Charles Street
Coburg North
VIC, 3058

CONTENTS

After practice, Tanner's soccer team was goofing around and talking about the latest viral video. He tried to join in, but Tanner never really "got" his teammates. Jon invited him over to play video games on Saturday. "I can't, I've got dance class," said Tanner.

"You're so gay, Tanner!" laughed Jon. Tanner didn't understand what dancing had to do with being gay. He knew his uncle was gay. He got married to his boyfriend last year. "I like dancing," said Tanner, making the rest of the team laugh a little and shake their heads.

Tanner loved playing soccer and he liked the guys on his team. But he fit in much better with his sister and her friends. They played soccer too, but were also interested in different things, like music and dance. Sometimes Tanner even dressed up, put on makeup, and did dance routines with the girls. The guys on the team would never understand!

Later that night, Tanner started worrying about what Jon said. What if dancing and wearing makeup means I'm gay? But if I'm gay, shouldn't I like boys more than I like girls? I don't get it.

Introduction
Confused

Like many young people, Tanner is often confused about how he fits in to the world. Fitting in might seem easy for some people, but Tanner is always **questioning his** gender identity **and** sexual orientation.

We start learning how to be boys and how to be girls when we're babies. It seems like there's a strict set of rules for boys and girls to follow. For example, boys are supposed to play football and girls are supposed to take dance lessons.

When we reach puberty, these rules get even more complicated. As our bodies develop, most of us start to think about sexuality and our feelings.

Society says that girls are supposed to think about boys and boys are supposed to think about girls. However, life is not that simple. The so-called rules about gender identity and sexual orientation don't always work.

"We learned about sex in school. The teacher told us that sex and gender aren't the same thing. Our genes make us who we are and everybody is unique. Some of us are girls and some are boys and some are in between." Ali, aged 10.

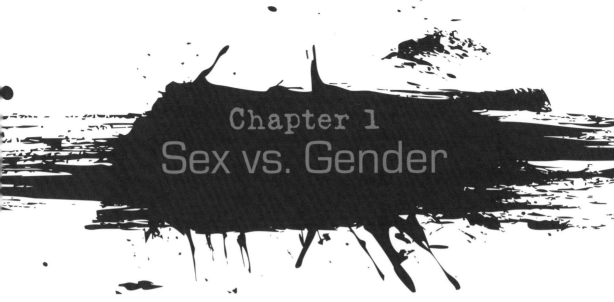

Chapter 1
Sex vs. Gender

There are girls and there are boys, right? The answer to this question is not as clear as it might seem. Everyone has both a **sex** and a **gender**. Sometimes they are the same and sometimes they are not.

Sex has to do with **biology**, or what our bodies are made of and how they work. Gender has to do with how we think and feel about ourselves within our culture. Our sex is defined by our **sexual organs**. Gender is about the behavior, interests, and other things that we think are "for boys" or "for girls."

Researchers aren't sure where gender comes from, but most think it's a combination of our feelings and our culture. For most people, sex and gender will be the same—a person born with the physical characteristics of a boy will mostly likely feel like a boy. The same is true for many girls. It's not true for everyone, though.

What's a Girl, What's a Boy?

Each person's biological sex depends on **DNA**. DNA is made up of **chromosomes**, or collections of genes. Genes are inherited characteristics, such as eye and hair color, that are passed down to new generations.

We get half of our chromosomes from our biological mothers and half from our biological fathers. We get an X sex chromosome from our mothers, and either an X or Y sex chromosome from our fathers. An X and a Y make a boy, and two Xs make a girl.

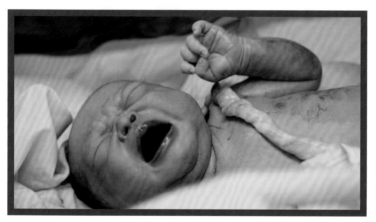

Many babies are born without a clearly defined sex.

Intersex

Not everyone is born a boy or a girl. About one in 2,000 babies are born without a clearly defined sex. As a result, many babies undergo surgeries to make their **genitals** appear male or female. The Intersex Society of North America suggests that parents wait until **intersex** children are old enough to decide for themselves if they want surgery.

The Gender Binary

Most people think of gender as being **binary**. In other words, there are only two options—male and female. **Advocates** are trying to change the way society views gender. They say there are many aspects to being male and female. Some people are a little bit of both.

Masculine or Feminine?

The words "male" and "female" refer to our sexes. But "masculine" and "feminine" describe the behaviors associated with each gender. Every culture has its own ideas about what women and men are supposed to be like. These ideas change over time. For example, we might describe a bicycle as a girl's bike if it is pink and has flowers on the basket. Our culture considers flowers and the color pink feminine.

Our ideas about what is "masculine" or "feminine" are changing every day.

"At my school the teachers don't make us line up as girls and boys, and we get to pick what people call us. There's a kid in a different class who was a girl but this year he gets to be a boy because he's a boy inside." Louisa, aged 16.

Chapter 2
Gender Identity and Expression

Sex is a biological fact and gender is how you feel inside. The way we understand gender is often based on social and cultural ideas about masculinity and femininity. Researchers don't know where gender comes from. It might be in our **nature**, the way we are **nurtured**, or a combination of the two.

Many researchers say girls behave like girls and boys behave like boys because of the way they are taught by their parents and communities. In other words, girls choose to play with dolls because people give them dolls.

This doesn't mean that we can turn a baby girl into a boy by treating her like a boy. Sometimes you can give a baby girl different toys and she'll still play with a doll. This is why some researchers believe genes decide gender before birth.

When you were younger, you might have played with members of the opposite sex more than you do now.

Gender Roles

The way we express our gender depends on the **gender roles** we are taught. We start learning about those roles right away. When we dress baby boys in blue clothes and baby girls in pink clothes, we assign them gender roles based on their sexes.

Usually people teach boys to be strong, athletic, and aggressive. Girls are taught to be quiet, sweet, and pretty. Adults often call boys "tiger" and "champ," and call girls "princess" and "darling."

What Happens at Recess?

What do you do at recess? When you were younger, you probably played together with all the kids in your class regardless of whether they were boys or girls. As you got older, you might have noticed that boys played more with boys, and girls played more with girls. Why do you think that happens?

Gender Roles through History

For most of history, the role of women has been one of wife and mother. This is because women give birth to babies and **nurse**, or breastfeed, them. Many so-called feminine characteristics are qualities that made women good wives and mothers such as being gentle.

Throughout history, leaders of nations have usually been men, with a few notable exceptions. That is why characteristics of good leaders, such as confidence and strength, are often seen as masculine. These gender roles led to **inequality** between the sexes. Men usually have more power and control than women have.

A Diverse World

Hundreds of years ago, Europeans moved to and took control of Africa, Asia, and the Americas. As they traveled, they spread their ideas of what gender roles should be. Before that time, many cultures had different ideas about the roles of men and women. In some Asian cultures, women and men did the same types of work. In some African cultures, women made the decisions for their communities.

In many societies, women work alongside men.

Gender Identity

We start learning about gender roles from our families before we even learn to talk. As we learn about gender roles and the personality traits that go with them, we start to identify the way we feel with a specific gender. Gender identity is how we feel about the gender we are supposed to be.

Sometimes when an intersex baby is born, parents and medical professionals decide which sex the baby should be. When they decide on a sex, they choose the same gender for that baby. That gender might not fit. An intersex person may be told he is a girl and be treated as a girl, but inside he knows that he's a boy. Consequently, this person identifies as a boy, even if his sex does not match.

Gender Expression

Gender expression is how we show gender identity to the world. Like gender roles, gender expression is defined by culture. If women are expected to wear dresses, then a person who identifies as a woman may want to wear dresses. As ideas of gender roles change, how we express gender changes too.

Different hairstyles, wearing makeup, and the clothes we wear are all expressions of gender. However, one of the most important ways to express gender is through pronouns. In English, the pronouns for females are "she" and "her." The pronouns for males are "he" and "him." The pronouns we use are labels for gender identity.

Breaking the Roles

History is full of people who did not follow traditional gender roles. For much of history, society has been dominated by males. However, some women refused to abide by those standards. Cleopatra in ancient Egypt, Joan of Arc in fifteenth-century France, and Queen Elizabeth I in the 1700s in England all took on roles of men in their societies.

Joan of Arc was a woman who did not follow traditional gender roles by leading men into battle.

Transgender

A person whose gender identity is different from the sex he or she was born with is considered transgendered. A transgendered person will often choose to express his or her true gender identity. Some transgendered people decide to transition, or change, their sex to match their gender. They do this through **hormone therapy** and surgery. A person who chooses to transition his or her sex is sometimes referred to as a "transsexual," but transgender is a more positive and **inclusive** term.

Sexual orientation has nothing to do with a person's biological sex.

What about Sexual Orientation?

Being transgendered has nothing to do with sexual orientation. Sexual orientation is based on how a person feels toward others, not on what their biological sex might be. If a transgendered person chooses to change his or her sex to match his or her gender, their sexual orientation would remain the same before and after that change.

A Third Gender?

Many native cultures in North America believe in a third gender. **Two-spirited** people share the characteristics of both male and female genders. These individuals have been accepted and well respected within Native American cultures for centuries.

In India, there is a group of people called the *hijra*. The hijra are male and intersex individuals who live as women. In Thailand the *kathoey* are men who dress and act as women. They are generally accepted in Thai society for who they are.

Common vs. Normal

Sometimes we think that uncommon things are **abnormal**. But "common" and "normal" are not the same thing. For example, red hair is uncommon, but having red hair is normal. If a person grew feathers out of his head instead of hair, that would be abnormal. Some people's gender identities are uncommon, but that doesn't mean they are abnormal.

In India, the hijra are men who live as women.

17

"The girls in my class talk about boys ALL the time.
There are some boys that I think I like. I think I
actually like girls. I guess that makes me a lesbian.
But...I don't know." Jen, aged 16.

Chapter 3
Sexual Orientation

Biology determines a person's sex. Gender identity is how he or she feels inside. Sexuality, however, is about attraction. Someone may be attracted to or romantically interested in men, women, both, or neither. This is called sexual orientation.

There are four basic types of sexual orientation: attraction to the opposite sex, attraction to the same sex, no sexual attraction to either sex, and attraction to both sexes. We can't predict who we are attracted to, nor can we choose who we are attracted to. It's a natural feeling inside of each individual.

How we define our sexual orientation usually has to do with our own gender. People attracted to the same sex have a homosexual orientation, while those attracted to the opposite sex are heterosexual.

What's a Homosexual?

The prefix "homo" means "the same" and the prefix "hetero" means "different." The term "homosexual" was first used to describe men who preferred romantic and sexual relationships with other men. Eventually, the term "heterosexual" was created to describe the relationships between men and women.

For many years, people used "homosexual" to identify men and women who were attracted to their own sex. Others used more insulting terms. People don't generally use the word "homosexual" anymore. "Gay" is the most common term. People often describe heterosexual men and women as "straight" or "hetero."

People of the same sex who are attracted to one another are commonly called "gay."

Gays and Lesbians

A gay person is homosexual because he or she is attracted to people of the same biological sex. A gay man seeks romantic relationships with other men. A gay woman, or lesbian, seeks romantic relationships with other women. Until recently, being gay was considered abnormal by many people. Those who were gay often pretended that they were not to avoid being shunned.

What's in a Name?

"Gay" is a word that means happy. Gay men first started using the word to describe themselves in the 1920s, but it took many years for everyone to use the term. Until then, gay men were usually described in negative ways. While the term gay can refer to both men and women, gay women are also identified as lesbians. The word "lesbian" comes from the Greek island of Lesbos. In ancient times, a female poet named Sappho lived there with a group of women and wrote about love between women.

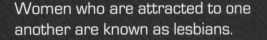

Women who are attracted to one another are known as lesbians.

Straight, Gay, or Both?

A person is considered **bisexual** when he or she is attracted to people of both sexes and genders. A bisexual person may have a romantic relationship with a man and later be in a romantic relationship with a woman. Many people think sexuality is flexible and that some people's attractions can change during their lifetime.

Romantic relationships are important for people of all sexual orientations.

A Private Matter

Starting a relationship with another person is one way to share one's sexual orientation with others. Even then, sexual orientation is still private. You might think a bisexual man is gay if he enters into a relationship with another man. There's no way to know a person's sexual orientation unless he or she tells you.

None of the Above

A person who is **asexual** does not have a strong attraction to any sex or gender. Asexual people are usually disinterested in sexual activity. It's difficult to know how many people identify as asexual. Asexual individuals may have romantic relationships because they want partners. Asexuality might seem unnatural to people of other sexual orientations, but it is part of the diversity of sexual orientation.

I Just Don't Know!

It's normal for preteens and teenagers to be confused about their sexuality. Some young people have a strong sense of both their gender identities and their sexual orientations. Others need time to work out how they feel. Some young people just aren't ready to think about it at all. There's no rush. Everyone is different. Even some adults take a long time to know themselves in this way.

It's normal to be confused about your sexuality.

GAYS AT School is SuPER Cool!!

"I helped to start the Gay-Straight Alliance at my school. A friend told me he was gay and that he wanted to come out. I wanted to help him. We asked our teacher to help us and we started the group. Only a few kids came to our first meetings. Now, tons of people come and we do lots of stuff. We're all about having a safe place for LGBTQ kids and allies at our school." Tiff, aged 15.

Chapter 4
Taking Action

When things have been a certain way for a long time, it takes the work of many brave people to make a change. Activists work to change old ways of thinking. They help to make the world better for everyone. Some of the earliest activists were **abolitionists** who fought to end slavery. Women and men also fought for equal rights for women and people of color.

Today, human rights activists fight for the rights of all people around the world, including the right of an individual to express his or her gender identity and sexual orientation without fear or judgment.

Lesbian, **g**ay, **b**isexual, and **t**ransgendered people, as well as those who are **q**uestioning their identities, form the **LGBTQ** community. There are different versions of this abbreviation. Sometimes letters for two-spirited, intersex, and asexual are added. LGBTQ activists also include **allies**, or people who are straight but who support LGBTQ rights.

Women's Rights Opened Our Eyes

Throughout history, women's rights movements helped societies understand that women can be and do many things. Wife and mother are no longer the only gender roles for women. Women can work the same jobs as men. Men can take care of children and their homes. This means that our understanding of gender roles has changed.

Gender Diversity

The change in gender roles has opened people's minds to new ideas. Today girls can play football and even box. Boys can take dance lessons without being teased. Yet, many people still believe that gender and sex are the same. While we might think gender roles are flexible, we still think that some things are just for girls and other things just for boys.

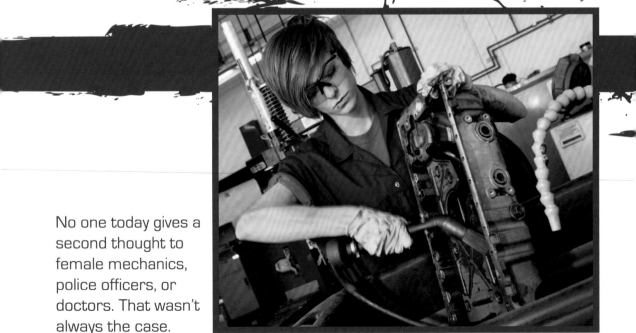

No one today gives a second thought to female mechanics, police officers, or doctors. That wasn't always the case.

LGBTQ Rights

The LGBTQ rights movement grew in the 1960s, when gay rights activists started advocating for all people whose gender identities or sexual orientation were less common. The LGBTQ rights movement now works to end **homophobia, transphobia,** and **discrimination.** They hope to encourage tolerance and acceptance. Changing laws is one way to protect LGBTQ people, but education and support are also important.

Violence of Hate

In 1998, a college student in Wyoming named Matthew Shepard was beaten and left to die. The men who killed him attacked Matthew because he was gay.

Matthew's death made ending violence against the LGBTQ community a priority across North America. His mother Judy became an activist and worked to make it a crime to harm a person because of his or her sexual identity. She and her husband Dennis started the Matthew Shepard Foundation. The goal of the group is to protect the rights of the LGBTQ community.

More than ten years after Matthew's death, the United States passed the Hate Crimes Prevention Act, also known as the Matthew Shepard Act. The act makes violence against LGBTQ people a hate crime, which can make punishment more severe.

Coming Out

Although society is changing, many LGBTQ people might not be comfortable sharing their identities with their communities, their families, and their friends. They might even deny it themselves. **Coming out** about sexual orientation or gender identity is a personal decision. You should never "out" another person, or share information about his or her sexual orientation or gender identity without permission.

Some kids and teenagers choose to come out, others do not. Parents might have a problem accepting that their child is different. Moreover, coming out at school, on a team, or even in a community can be scary. It's important that a person feels safe and has support before coming out. For some, coming out is easier to do when they are older and more independent. No one should ever feel pressured to come out. It may be helpful to come out to some people first and wait to tell others.

Deciding to come out is a personal decision that should be made when you think and feel the time is right.

Pride and Support

Each year, LGBTQ communities across the world hold Pride celebrations. A Pride parade is usually the focus of the festivities. Members of the LGBTQ community and their allies march to show that they are proud of who they are. Different community groups, businesses, and political leaders march to show their support for LGBTQ rights. Pride parades also include floats, music, and performers.

Many organizations support the LGBTQ community, including:

- **GLAAD** (pronounced "glad") is an American organization that focuses on how LGBTQ individuals are treated on TV, in music, in movies, and in the news.

- **PFLAG** (pronounced "pee-flag") is an organization of parents, friends, and allies of the LGBTQ community.

- **Egale** (pronounced "eh-gal") is a Canadian LGBTQ advocacy group that focuses on education and legal issues. The French word for "equal" is *égale*.

"My dads are gay. I know that both my dads love me, a lot. Most of my friends are cool about it. It's no big deal. This girl at my school has lesbian moms and a dad. Sometimes it's kind of hard not having a mom at all, but my dads are cool about stuff. And when I really want to talk about girl stuff, I just call my aunt." Gina, aged 13.

Chapter 5
Same-Sex Marriage and Families

Families with gay parents and children are becoming more common and accepted. However, some people still dislike the idea of gay people being parents. **Same-sex** or **gay marriage** is a very **controversial** topic. Many people disagree with allowing people of the same sex to marry.

Traditional ideas of marriage being between a man and a woman have existed for a long time. Marriage is also a religious act and many religions do not approve of sexual orientations other than heterosexuality.

Same-sex marriage laws are intended to allow gay people to be married legally. Under the law, a justice of the peace, a judge, or some other public official can legally marry a gay couple. However, the law does not force individual religions to marry same sex couples.

Why Same-Sex Marriage Matters

For many people, marriage is important. In most cultures, marriage is a commitment to love and live with another person and be a family. Married people share their lives and have children together. In the past, almost everyone got married. Today, some people choose not to marry but still commit to each other as a family. Allowing same-sex marriage gives gay people the right to make that choice.

Marriage is also a legal relationship in which married people have **obligations** to one other. Husbands and wives are expected to help each other and share the things they own. For example, married people have the legal right to make decisions for each other if one of them is very sick. And married people can inherit each other's property when a spouse dies. Supporters of gay marriage believe that same-sex couples should have the same legal rights as heterosexual married couples.

Many people in the United States want laws changed so gay people can marry.

Legal Status

Laws allowing same-sex marriage are very new. In 2001, the Netherlands became the first country to make same-sex marriage legal. In 2003, Ontario was the first place in Canada to allow same-sex marriage. By 2005, all of Canada allowed same-sex marriage.

In the United States, each state—not the federal government—make laws about marriage. In 2004, Massachusetts was the first U.S. state to make same-sex marriage legal. By the fall of 2014, 25 states, the District of Columbia, and 10 Native American tribal governments allowed same-sex marriages. Many additional states are reviewing their marriage laws.

What's a Civil Union?

A **civil union** is a legal partnership that gives two people many of the same rights as married couples. A civil union is not the same thing as a marriage, but it allows a couple to have a legal definition for their relationship. In many countries, allowing civil unions was the first step to making same-sex marriage legal.

Changing Families

You don't need a marriage certificate to have children. Families have undergone radical shifts in recent decades. Today, there are no rules for what makes a family. Families can be comprised of siblings, half-siblings, stepsiblings, foster parents, grandparents, aunts, uncles, godparents, guardians, girlfriends, boyfriends, and friends. Many kids have gay parents and many parents have gay children.

It's easier today for families to be open about their relationships and identities, but that doesn't mean LGBTQ families never existed before. Many celebrities are sharing their own personal stories. Actress Jenna Malone, who starred in *The Hunger Games: Catching Fire*, was raised by her mother and her mother's girlfriend. Rapper Jay-Z's mother is gay, and he is a strong advocate for LGBTQ rights.

Families have undergone a radical shift from the traditional family of mother, father, and children.

Many Ways to Make a Family

The right for LGBTQ individuals to **adopt** children is important. In partner or stepparent adoption, a person can legally adopt the children of his or her partner. In joint adoption, couples or individuals can adopt a child who does not have parents. In Canada, all types of adoption are legal for

The actor Neil Patrick Harris (left) and his husband are the fathers of twins.

LGBTQ parents. Some U.S. states still restrict one type or both types of adoption by LGBTQ parents.

There are many other ways to start a family. Some LGBTQ individuals become parents through previous relationships with the opposite sex. Lesbians can use a **sperm donor** to make babies. Gay men can have babies with the help of a **surrogate mother**. Broadway and TV star Neil Patrick Harris and his husband had twins with the help of a surrogate. TV star Sara Gilbert had two children with her female partner.

"I always wear a pink shirt to school on anti-bullying day. The Pink Shirt Day thing started when this older student heard about a boy at his school who was bullied because he wore a pink shirt. The bullies were saying he was gay, or something. The next day the older guy and his friends all wore pink shirts. Everybody in my school--all the girls and the boys--wears a pink shirt on Pink Shirt Day." Jodi, aged 14.

Chapter 6
A Changing Society

Society is learning to accept different gender identities and sexual orientations. Same-sex marriage and LGBTQ families are just two examples. But it can be difficult for adults to change their long-held opinions. Kids are much more open to new ideas. Young people are paving the way for change in our world.

Expressing Gender Identity

In 2013, an 11-year-old boy named Wren came out as transgendered. He was born a girl, but he identified as a boy when he was four. His parents ignored it at first, but eventually his little sister told his mother that Wren "really is a boy."

Wren's parents decided to let him live as a boy. He started school as a boy—only his teachers and his friends' parents knew that his sex was female. When he started the seventh grade, he decided to go public about being a transgendered boy. His schoolmates were very accepting.

Many groups, including the Girl Scouts, are coming to terms with how people define their gender.

Bobby's Story

In 2011, a young girl in Colorado named Bobby wanted to join the Girl Scouts. At first, the Girl Scouts turned her away because her sex was male, even though Bobby dressed like a girl and played with girls' toys. Her parents complained and eventually the Girl Scouts announced that if you consider yourself a girl and your parents treat you as a girl, it's okay to become a Girl Scout.

A Goal for Jesse

In 2014, a young transgender hockey player named Jesse challenged the changeroom policy in Ontario, Canada. He wasn't allowed to change with the rest of his team in the boys' room. He also wasn't welcome in the girls' changeroom.

Jesse won his case and now all youth hockey players in Ontario must be allowed to use the changeroom that matches their gender identities.

No Gender? No Problem!

In 2011, a family in Toronto, Canada, decided not to reveal the sex of their newborn baby. At the time, their 6-year-old son, Jazz, didn't behave the way little boys were expected to act. Jazz

Youth hockey leagues in Ontario must accommodate transgender players.

liked wearing dresses, having long hair, and the color pink. Some people thought that Jazz was being a strange little boy, and other people thought he was actually a girl.

When Jazz's parents had their third child, Storm, in 2011, they didn't want other people to treat this baby as if he was a boy or a girl. Instead of telling Storm to be a girl or a boy, they decided to let Storm express his or her gender naturally. When the family's story appeared in the news, people all over the world criticized their decision. Three years later, Storm was a happy child who still hadn't selected a gender. Storm's parents were content with their decision.

"I watch YouTube videos a lot. When I have a bad day at school and people make fun of me, I watch these videos about people who are gay and trans...it makes me think about stuff. It's really hard at school and sometimes I feel like I just want to stop living. I talked to my teacher and she told me about the videos. They make me feel better sometimes."
Chris, aged 15.

Chapter 7
It Gets Better

Even though society is changing, life can still be very difficult for LGBTQ adults, kids, and teens. It's not easy feeling as though you don't fit in. Being LGBTQ can be very lonely, confusing, and sometimes scary. And if your friends and family don't support you, those feelings can get even worse.

People who are LGBTQ may be afraid that their families will not accept them. Some communities are more traditional than others and are afraid of change.

Some religions have a very rigid understanding of sex and gender. These religions do not welcome gays or lesbians into their churches. Kids whose parents and family don't support the LGBTQ community may not be supportive of LGBTQ peers.

Sticks and Stones

Some people use very hurtful words to identity people who are LGBTQ. If you use these words, you are telling the world that you think being LGBTQ is a bad thing. However, the LGBTQ community has taken many labels, such as "queer" and "dyke," and made them their own. Now that "gay" is used as a positive word, saying "that's so gay" when something is uncool just doesn't make sense!

Dangers: Homelessness and Suicide

Experts estimate that around 10 percent of young people in North America are LGBTQ. However, somewhere between 20 and 40 percent of homeless youth are LGBTQ. Many of them run away from home because of family conflicts or abuse. LGBTQ youth on the street are more likely to be the victims of violence than other homeless youth.

Suicide is another danger facing LGBTQ youth. In the United States, suicide is the third most common cause of death for young people. In Canada, it ranks second. At least one quarter of LGBTQ teens attempt suicide. Based on these statistics, it's likely that suicide is the main cause of death for LGBTQ teens in North America.

Homelessness is a major problem for young people who are LGBTQ.

It Gets Better

In 2010, writer and activist Dan Savage and his partner Terry Miller started the It Gets Better project. That year, there were many news stories of teens who killed themselves after being bullied because they were LGBTQ—or their bullies thought that they were.

It Gets Better asked happy and successful LGBTQ adults to tell their stories on video and post them to YouTube. The goal was to show young people facing tough times that life gets better. Many of those who made the videos talked about how difficult it was when they were young. More than 200 videos were made in the first week. There are now more than 50,000 videos on the It Gets Better website. Savage and Miller also published a book of It Gets Better messages from LGBTQ adults and allies.

If you think you're alone, remember you're not. There are many people in the LGBTQ community.

I don't like hanging out with other girls or like the things they like. Does that mean I'm supposed to be a boy?

A: No. People who are transgender have a very strong feeling inside. The things you like to do don't define your gender. You may not fit into the gender roles you see around you right now, but that's okay. Be the person you are—as you grow older, you'll see that there are many ways to be a woman or a man. If you're confused, talk to an adult you trust about how you're feeling.

I have weird feelings towards my best friend who is the same sex that I am. Does that mean I'm gay?

A: Maybe. Maybe not. During puberty, boys can have very strong sexual feelings that have nothing to do with any one person or type of person. Girls often have very strong feelings about their best friends.

There's no rush to label your sexual orientation. Sexual identity develops over time and will start to make more sense as you get a little older. If you can, talk to an adult you trust about how you're feeling.

My parents tease me and my sisters about liking boys. They always talk about how I'm going to get married some day and have a family. They're going to be so upset if I tell them I might be gay. What should I do?

A: Just like you, your parents and family live in a world where most people's gender identity matches their sex. They may not have even thought about the possibility that you might be LGBTQ. When you're ready to tell them, you may be surprised at how understanding and accepting they are. It may take them time to get used to the idea.

My older brother told my parents he wanted to be a girl. My mother cried. My dad got really angry and got into a fight with my brother and hit him. My brother ran away and I'm scared.

A: First, if you are in danger, you should tell an adult you trust right away. You can also call the phone numbers in the next section of this book for help. If you are in contact with your brother, tell him about the resources listed in this book so he can get help too.

My parents got divorced and now my mom has a girlfriend. She's really nice and I like her a lot. But next summer they are going to get married and I'm afraid to tell the kids at school.

A: First, tell your mom about your fears. She can help you figure out what to do. You may want to start by telling your best friends first. Your mom may also want to talk to your teachers and your friends' parents. Every situation is different, but the important thing is to work together as a family. Create a plan for how you're going to talk about your family and what to do if other people are mean or bully you.

Other Resources

The following websites and hotlines will provide you with trustworthy information about sexual orientation and gender identity.

It Gets Better
www.itgetsbetter.org
An online video campaign that provides support to LGBTQ youth.

In the United States

Advocates for Youth
www.advocatesforyouth.org
An organization that helps young people make choices about their sexual health.

GLBT National Help Center
www.glbtnationalhelpcenter.org
The oldest national organization that provides information and support to LGBTQ youth and adults.

GSA Network
www.gsanetwork.org
A national online resource for Gay-Straight Alliance student groups.

Trans Lifeline

www.translifeline.org/

1-877-565-8860

This helpline helps transgender individuals in crisis.

The Trevor Project

www.thetrevorproject.org

1-866-4-U-TREVOR (1-866-488-7386)

If you are considering suicide or need help, call the 24-hour Trevor Project now.

In Canada

Lesbian Gay Bi Trans Youth Line

www.youthline.ca

1-800-268-YOUTH (9688)

A peer hotline where you can talk to other kids about your questions and get more information about the LGBTQ community.

My GSA

www.mygsa.ca

An online resource for Gay-Straight Alliances across Canada run by Egale.

Kids Help Phone

www.kidshelpphone.ca

1-800-668-6868

If you are considering suicide or need help, call the 24-hour Kids Help Phone now.

Trans Lifeline

www.translifeline.org/

1-877-330-6366

This helpline helps transgender individuals in crisis.

Glossary

Note: Words appearing in boldface but not in the glossary have been explained in the text.

abnormal The opposite of normal

adopt To legally take in another person's child and raise it as part of your family

advocate A person who pleads the cause of another

chromosomes The parts of a cell that contain the genes which control how an animal or plant grows and what it becomes

coming out Telling other people about your gender identity

controversial Dispute over opposing views

discrimination Unfair treatment of a person because of his or her sex, gender, race, religion, age, or ability

DNA Material found in cells that contain genetic information

gender The emotional, behavioral, and cultural characteristics attached to a person's biological sex

gender identity How a person feels about their gender and biological sex

gender roles The social expectations of how people should act, think, or feel based on their biological sex

genitals The sexual organs outside of our bodies, including the penis and the vagina

homophobia Fear and hatred of gay people

hormone therapy Use of drugs to suppress the production of, or inhibit, a hormone

inclusive To include many kinds

inequality An unfair difference in situation

intersex A biological sex that is not completely male or completely female

nature The features of a person or thing that won't change

nurture To care for something to help it grow and develop

obligations Things that you have to do

puberty The time of life when children develop into teenagers

same-sex or gay marriage Marriage between two men or two women

sex The biological categories of male and female

sexual organs Body parts related to the reproductive system

sexual orientation Attracted to one particular sex

sperm donor A male who provides sperm for the purpose of impregnating a woman who is not his sexual partner

surrogate mother A women who carries a baby and gives birth for another person

transphobia Fear and hatred of transgendered people

two-spirited Having the characteristics of both male and female genders

Index

48